THE
EMOTIONAL INTELLIGENCE
POCKETBOOK

By Margaret Chapman

Drawings by Phil Hailstone

"Loaded with practicality; you will be inspired to use your emotions in ways that make you healthier, happier and more productive."
Dr. Hendrie Weisinger, author *Emotional Intelligence at Work.*

"More than a pocket snack, this is a highly recommended and fulfilling appetiser to a life-enriching feast. Margaret has used her EI well."
Sir John Whitmore, author *Coaching for Performance.*

CONTENTS

CONTENTS

ACKNOWLEDGEMENTS
This book is the outcome of three years' work in which I have been submerged in an emerging field of interest in management, leadership and personal development. There are many who have directly and indirectly informed my thinking and feelings about the subject. I want to thank the many managers with whom I have worked on a 1:1 basis, helping them to build their EI; to research participants, whose insights have served to fuel my continued enthusiasm; and to facilitators whose courses have contributed to my own skills and EI development. Specifically I would like to thank Dr Hank Weisinger, whose seminal work inspired the 5-step model, and my partner, Robin Clarke, who developed the Boston EIQ from his own research into the emotional intelligence of police officers.

Published by:
Management Pocketbooks Ltd
Laurel House, Station Approach, Alresford, Hants SO24 9JH, U.K.
Tel: +44 (0)1962 735573   Fax: +44 (0)1962 733637
E-mail: sales@pocketbook.co.uk
Website: www.pocketbook.co.uk

This edition published 2001. Reprinted 2002, 2003, 2004, 2005, 2006, 2007.

© Margaret Chapman 2001

British Library Cataloguing-in-Publication Data – A catalogue record for this book is available from the British Library.

ISBN   978 1 870471 95 4

Design, typesetting and graphics by Efex Ltd.   Printed in U.K.

INTRODUCTION

IMPACT OF ORGANISATIONAL CHANGE

It was Aristotle who spoke about a rare ability *to be angry with the right person, to the right degree, at the right time, for the right purpose and in the right way.*

How prophetic his words. Everything we know about organisations has changed. Once, working life was stable but a whole new lexicon has developed that includes such euphemisms as downsizing, rightsizing, delayering and restructuring to describe the present state of chaos and complexity.

These new organisational realities mean that managers are being judged by a new yardstick. To be successful you don't just need to be intelligent, you need to be emotionally intelligent.

HOW OTHERS SEE IT

> *Without a doubt I know managers who are not emotionally intelligent and they are not very effective ... they are not good people managers ... they are not particularly good at their jobs ... and they are certainly not the excelling managers that I would be looking at as my role models. The people who are emotionally aware, in my experience, are the people who get the most from you ... will help you to develop ... and ultimately put you in a position to help other people.*
> Young high-flier, major private sector organisation

> *For leadership positions emotional intelligence competencies account for up to 85% of what sets outstanding managers apart from the average.*
> Daniel Goleman, *Working with Emotional Intelligence*, 1998

AIMS OF THIS POCKETBOOK

This book is designed to:

- Introduce emotional intelligence (EI) by defining what it is and explaining why it is important
- Provide a framework for understanding EI
- Illustrate ways in which to begin to develop your EI capabilities
- Offer you an opportunity to assess your EI
- Stimulate reflection on the changing nature of organisations and your role as a manager
- Outline guidelines on how to use EI as an organisational change management strategy

This book is designed for:

- Managers who recognise that being an effective leader is about *inside-out* development
- Human resource practitioners who want a short guide to this popular concept and some practical tools which they can use to begin to develop their own EI

WHAT THE BOOK IS NOT

This book is not a definitive guide to what is a rapidly growing field. It is designed as a route map, with signposts for those who want to pursue their EI journey further. Much has been written about emotional intelligence but little that is readily accessible to the informed practitioner or manager with limited time available to trawl through heavyweight literature.

I have done that for you and my hopes in writing this book are that it will inspire, inform and encourage you to continue on your EI travels and enjoy the benefits of an emotionally intelligent life.

OBLIVION   EI THIS WAY

WHAT IS EMOTIONAL INTELLIGENCE?

It depends on whom you ask. The original theory of emotional intelligence was developed by two U.S. psychologists, Peter Salovey and John Mayer in 1990 who defined this as a learned ability to perceive, understand and express our feelings accurately and to control our emotions so that they work for us, not against us.

In other words, no matter whose definition you use, EI is about:

- Knowing how you and others feel and what to do about it

- Knowing what feels good and what feels bad and how to get from bad to good

- Possessing emotional awareness, sensitivity and the skills that will help us to stay positive and maximise our long-term happiness and well-being

Dr Hendrie Weisinger suggests this is simply using our emotions intelligently!

INTRODUCTION

WHY EMOTIONAL INTELLIGENCE NOW?

Whilst it was Salovey and Mayer who gave us the original theory of EI and coined the phrase emotional intelligence, it was the work of Daniel Goleman in 1996 and 1998 that really put 'EQ' on the organisational map. My research shows that some of the reasons for this popularity include:

- Changing nature of work: flatter structures, fewer tiers of management, greater responsibility
- Increasing complexity: impact of technology and reshaping of jobs
- Rising competition: shorter product life-cycles and more demanding customers
- Globalisation of markets: organisations now need to think global, yet act local
- Rapid pace of change: change is now a constant feature of organisational life
- Rising stress levels: the World Health Organisation predicts that depression will be the second highest cause of death in the next 10 years (stress is a mild form of depression)
- Redefining what it means to be a success: not simply what we do, but who we are – what Goleman calls being judged by a new 'yardstick'
- Increasing emphasis on performance – particularly that of leaders: again voicing one of my research participants, "EI is all about leadership" that is IQ = EQ = success
- Zeitgeist: a sign of the times – we talk more about emotions now

INTRODUCTION

WHY BOTHER TO DEVELOP YOUR EI?

The business case for emotional intelligence – US research:

- Partners in a multi-national consulting firm were assessed on EI; those high on EI secured $1.2 million more profit

- Analysis of 300+ top executives showed certain EI competencies (influence, team leadership, organisational awareness, self-confidence) distinguished star performers

- National insurance company agents weak on EI sold average policies of $54,000; sales agents high on EI achieved $114,000

- The Centre for Creative Leadership identified that the primary cause of career derailment amongst top executives was the lack of EI

- Of the sales representatives at a computer company hired on EI, 90% were more likely to finish training

Source: www.eiconsortium.org

WHY BOTHER TO DEVELOP YOUR EI?

Recent UK research:

- A survey of managers in a UK supermarket chain revealed those with high EI experienced less stress, enjoyed better health, performed better and reported a better life/work balance (UMIST, 2001)

- Police officers who are able to identify and manage emotions report lower levels of stress (Goldsmiths College, London, 2000)

- Public Sector Housing Officers report greater levels of cohesion, collaboration and sense of identity following team EI intervention (Chapman, 2004; 2005)*

* Contact **mc@eicoaching.co.uk** for copy articles

9

WHY BOTHER TO DEVELOP YOUR EI?

Still need more evidence? The hard case for soft skills:

- The Harvard School of Public Health predicts that by 2020 depression will be responsible for more lost workdays in the developed world than heart disease
- When corporations hire MBAs the three most desired competencies are: communication skills, interpersonal skills and initiative
- Two-thirds of stress-related problems result from *abusive, unsatisfying, limiting or ill-defined relationships*
- In the EU 8% of employees have faced bullying
- In 1997 the American Medical Association found that physicians who lack empathy get sued more often
- Assertiveness, empathy, happiness, emotional self-awareness and problem-solving skills are more predictive of sales success than background, gender and sales techniques
- Studies of 500 organisations worldwide indicate that people who score highest on EI measures rise to the top of organisations

Source: Fenman, *Using Emotional Intelligence at Work*

THE FIVE STEPS TO
EMOTIONAL INTELLIGENCE

FIVE-STEP MODEL

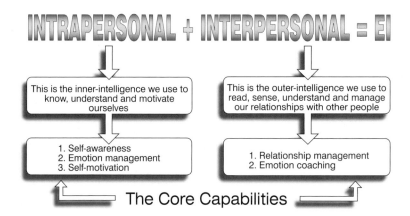

INTRAPERSONAL + INTERPERSONAL = EI

This is the inner-intelligence we use to know, understand and motivate ourselves

This is the outer-intelligence we use to read, sense, understand and manage our relationships with other people

1. Self-awareness
2. Emotion management
3. Self-motivation

1. Relationship management
2. Emotion coaching

The Core Capabilities

MODEL APPROACH

As the model opposite shows, to become
emotionally intelligent you have to develop both
your intrapersonal and interpersonal
intelligence. You do this by focusing on five
core capabilities, each one taking you a
step closer towards EI.

This chapter looks at each of those
capabilities in turn, starting with
self-awareness which, along with
emotion management and *self-motivation*, is central to your
intrapersonal intelligence – the
inner-intelligence we use to know,
understand and motivate ourselves.

THE FIVE STEPS TO EMOTIONAL INTELLIGENCE

STEP 1: SELF-AWARENESS

There is only one corner of the universe that you can be certain of improving; and that is your own self.
Aldous Huxley

THE FIVE STEPS TO EMOTIONAL INTELLIGENCE

STEP 1: SELF-AWARENESS

Self-awareness is the ability to see ourselves with our own eyes, to be aware of our ...

- Goals, immediate and long-term
- Beliefs, about ourselves and others
- Values, those things we hold dear
- Drivers, that affect how we work
- Rules, that we live by, the *shoulds, musts* and *oughts*
- Self-talk, the inner voice that tells us we *can* or *cannot* do something

... and the ways in which these impact on what we do and contribute to our *map of the world.*

Often, some of our inner drives are hidden from our consciousness. Emotional intelligence enables us to access this information by helping us to tune into our responses and identify our *hot buttons* – those core beliefs and values – which, if pressed, evoke the *flight* or *fight* response, trigger an emotion and propel us into action, for good or bad!

THE FIVE STEPS TO EMOTIONAL INTELLIGENCE

STEP 1: SELF-AWARENESS

WHO AM I AS A MANAGER?
INTERNAL AND EXTERNAL DIMENSIONS

Source: adapted from *Why EQ Matters for Consultants and Developers,* Organisations & People, Vol.7, No.1, Dyke, Martin & Woollard, 1999

THE FIVE STEPS TO EMOTIONAL INTELLIGENCE

STEP 1: SELF-AWARENESS

EXAMPLE

Let's look at an example:

You have been asked to carry out a particularly difficult project usually given to more experienced colleagues. You feel valued, trusted and excited. You are also a little anxious *(your self-talk tells you that you are not good enough)*.

Whilst working hard on the project your emotions swing from elation and joy to fear and frustration.

You achieve the task on time and within budget. You feel relieved and proud. You tell your boss and show her your completed work. Your boss gives you no thanks or praise and picks up a minor fault.

You then feel angry and decide that you are never again going to put yourself out. You feel exploited *(self-talk clicks in to reinforce your belief that you weren't good enough)*.

You think about leaving the company *(one of your beliefs is that hard work should be valued and that has been challenged)*. You begin to feel disappointed and upset. You update your résumé and begin to look at the vacancy section.

THE FIVE STEPS TO EMOTIONAL INTELLIGENCE

STEP 1: SELF-AWARENESS

How can you begin to identify the filters (hot buttons)
that trigger your emotions, and use this information
positively to change events (such as those in our
example) and achieve a more positive outcome?

You can identify your emotional responses by:
- Tuning into your senses
- Getting in touch with your feelings
- Knowing your goals

THE FIVE STEPS TO EMOTIONAL INTELLIGENCE

STEP 1: SELF-AWARENESS
TUNING INTO YOUR SENSES

This means paying attention to what you see and hear and not what you think you see and hear. Your beliefs, values, drivers and rules act as filters, distorting and deleting what otherwise might be important information. A lyric by Simon & Garfunkel in the song 'The Boxer' describes this process perfectly, *We see what we want to see and disregard the rest*.

For example, going back to the scenario with your boss, did she actually pick up on a minor error or was that just your perception? What information did you use to make this appraisal: how she looked or something she did or said that you could have misinterpreted? Alternatively, perhaps some hot button was pushed that triggered what Daniel Goleman calls an *emotional hijacking*, ie: the bypassing of information from our higher *thinking brain* directly to our (older and less developed) *emotional brain* whose evolutionary purpose is survival.

All too often our filters get in the way of information that hits our senses. The higher your level of self-awareness, the greater your ability to recognise and distinguish between what is fact and what is the result of a filter.

THE FIVE STEPS TO EMOTIONAL INTELLIGENCE

STEP 1: SELF-AWARENESS

TUNING INTO YOUR SENSES

The Map Is Not The Territory
(Alfred Korzybski, *Science & Sanity*, 1933)

People act from their map
as opposed to *reality*.
Different maps of the same
reality are of equal value,
depending on context.
Recognise your map and
you open up infinite
possibilities of seeing
the world in new ways.

Source: figure adapted
from The NLP Basic Training
Collection Manual Advanced
Neuro Dynamics

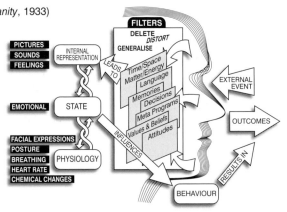

THE FIVE STEPS TO EMOTIONAL INTELLIGENCE

STEP 1: SELF-AWARENESS

 EXERCISE: GAUGING THE MOOD

Now let's try something practical. When you are next in a meeting at work, assess the mood of the group by simply relying on sensory information – what you see and hear.

Seeing:

- Pay attention to how people look at one another whilst they are speaking or listening. Do they look each other straight in the eye (which may indicate confidence)?

- Does the speaker look at everyone or just focus on one individual? (The former could reflect comfort with the group as a whole and a sense of the group being a team.)

- Do listeners stay focused or do their eyes wander? (The former suggests interest in what is being said, the latter indicates lack of interest.)

- Do you see people smile, smirk, frown or glare?

THE FIVE STEPS TO EMOTIONAL INTELLIGENCE

STEP 1: SELF-AWARENESS

 EXERCISE: GAUGING THE MOOD (Cont'd)

Hearing:

- Tune into the sounds in the room, people's voices.

- When a person speaks, is there quiet except for the person's voice or do you hear people moving in their chairs? (The former suggests interest, the latter perhaps boredom.)

- Do people speak stridently (this might reflect anger or frustration) or hesitantly (this might reflect a lack of knowledge of the subject)?

- Do you hear a lot of mumbled conversations while someone is talking? (This could indicate enthusiasm with what the person has to say and eagerness among individuals to comment further. Or, could it denote disapproval, with individuals expressing their disagreement to colleagues?)

- Do people yell or whisper, moan or interrupt?

THE FIVE STEPS TO EMOTIONAL INTELLIGENCE

STEP 1: SELF-AWARENESS

EXERCISE: GAUGING THE MOOD (Cont'd)

At the end of the meeting, look at all the information you have collected and see what you can deduce about the mood of the group, based solely on this information.

- Was the team enthusiastic?
- Did they seem pleased that management was willing to try some new idea?
- Did they appear to want to work together as a group to implement the changes?
- Did they all appear to grasp the importance of making the changes?

This exercise shows how sensory information can be used to influence your assessments. Being aware of how this happens enables you to rely more on your senses and therefore establish more accurate assessments. It helps you to move from what you *think* you see, to what you *actually* observe.

Source: adapted from *Emotional Intelligence at Work*, Hendrie Weisinger

THE FIVE STEPS TO EMOTIONAL INTELLIGENCE

STEP 1: SELF-AWARENESS

GETTING IN TOUCH WITH YOUR FEELINGS

Within psychology there has been a great deal of debate about the exact nature of an emotion. For our purposes, an emotion can be seen to consist of four elements:

1. What we think   – our interpretation of events that produces a particular emotional response or thought

2. What we feel   – a label that we use to describe a particular state

3. How our bodies react   – eg: racing heartbeat, feeling tense

4. How we behave   – eg: running away, hitting out or hugging someone

It is generally accepted that an emotion is not simply an automatic physical response to a situation, but our interpretation of bodily changes and information available to us.

THE FIVE STEPS TO EMOTIONAL INTELLIGENCE

STEP 1: SELF-AWARENESS
GETTING IN TOUCH WITH YOUR FEELINGS

Although our feelings are internal, they are often accompanied by outward (often physical) manifestations. By paying attention to these external signals, you can begin to understand what these feelings mean for you, moment by moment.

For example:
- Butterflies in the stomach may mean excitement or fear
- Glowing face may mean embarrassment
- Relaxing into a chair may mean that you are at ease

Certain feelings drive particular behaviours. By retracing the link between a physical response, your interpretation and the feeling, you can begin to identify your emotional responses in any given situation. One way in which you can develop this capability is to record changes in your emotional state by keeping a *feeling* diary.

THE FIVE STEPS TO EMOTIONAL INTELLIGENCE

STEP 1: SELF-AWARENESS

GETTING IN TOUCH WITH YOUR FEELINGS

Keeping a feeling diary helps you identify your emotional responses. When you notice your mood change, ask yourself: *What is going through my mind right now?* And, as soon as possible, write down your mental image or thought in the *Automatic thought(s)* column.

Date/ Time	Automatic thought(s) What did you think?	Emotion(s) How did you feel?	Response What did you do?	Outcome(s) What were consequences?
	Describe: • Actual event • Stream of thoughts, daydream or recollections leading to the emotions • Any physical sensations	Write down: • Thoughts that preceded the emotion(s)	Specify: • Emotion (eg: sadness, anxiety, happiness)	Detail: • What happened
Example Mon 18th 0930	• Presentation to the Board on new product launch • *I've really not had enough time to prepare, boss dropped this on me at last minute, we are not ready* • Stomach churning, pressure building at back of neck	• She (boss) should have done this presentation • I'm going to blow it; I know the Finance Director has it in for me • They are going to see it's not clearly thought through; it will be my fault • I'll look a fool	• Anxiety • Fear	• Just managed to get through • Board not entirely convinced • Asked to re-present in a month

THE FIVE STEPS TO EMOTIONAL INTELLIGENCE

STEP 1: SELF-AWARENESS

GETTING IN TOUCH WITH YOUR FEELINGS

Now, thinking about the example, consider the following questions:

1. What is the evidence that the automatic thought is true? Or not true? *In our hectic business lives today, is there ever enough time or do we do the best that we can within the time available?*
2. Could there be an alternative explanation? *What is the evidence that the boss 'dropped' him in it?*
3. What is the worst that could happen? *Further work needed? (Is this so awful?)*
4. What's the best that could happen? *That the Board don't throw out the ideas altogether.*
5. What should I do about it? *Use it as a learning opportunity.*
6. What is the effect of my believing the automatic thoughts? *Negative thinking evokes an 'emotional hijacking' and undermines performance.*
7. What could be the effect of changing my thinking? *You feel positive, knowing that you have done your best and believe in the work the team has done and what you've got to say.*
8. If you were in this situation, what would you think/feel/do?

THE FIVE STEPS TO EMOTIONAL INTELLIGENCE

STEP 1: SELF-AWARENESS
GETTING IN TOUCH WITH YOUR FEELINGS

Let's take another look at the example:

Date/Time	Automatic thought(s) What did you think?	Emotion(s) How did you feel?	Response What did you do?	Outcome(s) What were consequences?
Example Mon 18th 0930	• Presentation to the Board on new product launch • *Ideally, boss should do it, but something urgent must have come up* • *Short notice but done my best within time available* • Slight churning in stomach	• Boss given some steer on key players • Finance Director key stakeholder; need to focus on influencing him • Team has worked hard and I really believe in our approach • Feel positive	• Adrenalin pumping, to be expected • Feel anxious but I am going to knock them dead	• Presentation went great • Got the go-ahead to move to launch date (Finance Director particularly convinced by cost-benefit analysis)

THE FIVE STEPS TO EMOTIONAL INTELLIGENCE

STEP 1: SELF-AWARENESS

KNOWING YOUR GOALS

Our goals are what spur us into action. These might be short-term (what we want to accomplish right now/next month) or longer-term (for example, what we would like to have done with our lives).

As with our feelings, our desires or intentions are not always obvious to us. The value of becoming aware of our goals is that we can use this information to help us develop the strategies necessary to get what we really, really want.

For example, suppose you receive a call from an associate who asks you to stand in for him on a project in a week's time. You've recently freed up your diary to write a conference paper, so you could physically do it. However, do you:

- Agree but feel guilty because you have moved other commitments out of your schedule to focus on your writing?

- Say *no* because you have commitments?

- Say *possibly* and leave it vague – you will see what you can do and then get back to him (saying *no*)

THE FIVE STEPS TO EMOTIONAL INTELLIGENCE

STEP 1: SELF-AWARENESS

KNOWING YOUR GOALS

If you decide that:

1. You want to impress your associate with your ability to help out (despite obvious costs to yourself) you will say *yes*
2. You recognise the importance of producing work that is going to contribute to increasing your profile – for long-term success – you will say *no*
3. You want to demonstrate your concern, but really want to say *no*, maybe you will think how both your needs and his can be satisfied

What are the implications?

1. In the first case your underlying motives might be the need to achieve approval
2. In the second, you have a clear sense of direction and what your goals are, and you are prepared to assert your needs to achieve these
3. In the third, you are engaging in avoidance behaviour

What would **you** do?

THE FIVE STEPS TO EMOTIONAL INTELLIGENCE

STEP 1: SELF-AWARENESS

TIPS FOR IDENTIFYING YOUR GOALS

Here are some tips for identifying your goals:

Believe your behaviour
When we are enthusiastic about something, it is because we **want** to do it. If you are delaying getting started or avoiding a task, ask yourself if this is something you really want to be doing. Listen to the answer and observe your behaviour. This might reveal your true intentions. For example, agreeing to stand in for your associate might give the impression that you are dependable and supportive, but at what costs to your own needs? (How long before you get back to him to say *no*?)

Trust your feelings
When you feel happy, satisfied or content in a certain situation, it is likely that you are in alignment with your inner- and outer-self, ie: you are doing what you **want** to be doing (referred to as being congruent). However, if you have agreed to undertake something and you feel resentment, it could well be that your original intention is in conflict with some underlying goal. For example, in the scenario with your associate, you may have agreed to help him out, but begin to feel angry at his demands. In this case, your real intention was to say *no* and focus on what you **really wanted** to do (ie: write your paper).

THE FIVE STEPS TO EMOTIONAL INTELLIGENCE

STEP 1: SELF-AWARENESS
TIPS FOR IDENTIFYING YOUR GOALS (Cont'd)

Be honest with yourself
Are you harbouring any hidden agendas? For example,
securing a much sought after promotion may not be
what you really want, but is simply an opportunity to
impress your colleagues and friends. You might even
be running *parent-tapes* – voices of authority from the
past that prompt you to behave in certain ways. They
may have served you well as a child, but are not always
helpful or effective for you as an adult. (Like agreeing to
stand in for your associate because of your need for
external approval?)

Finding out who you are, where you have come from and
why you are here, can provide the map for finding your
path with a heart – a journey that harnesses your passion and
energies and yields that *feel-good* factor. Remember, if we don't
know where we are going, we may end up somewhere else!

THE FIVE STEPS TO EMOTIONAL INTELLIGENCE

STEP 1: SELF-AWARENESS

SETTING YOUR GOALS

Steps to setting exceptional goals and finding *your path with a heart:*

1. State your goal in the positive (what you want rather than don't want)
2. Own it
3. Make it sensory specific (What will it feel like when you have achieved your goal? What will it sound like? What will it look like?)
4. Check the ecology (Is it something you really, really want? What or who else might be affected when you have achieved your goal?)
5. Identify the resources you need and go for it!

This can be remembered by using what Julie Hay refers to as **POSIE**:

P ositive statement

O wned by the initiator (you)

S ensory-based

I ntention preserved (What will you gain or lose?)

E cology check (Remember, we exist in a system, family, friends, work: if you achieve your outcome, what or who else might be affected?)

THE FIVE STEPS TO EMOTIONAL INTELLIGENCE

STEP 2: EMOTION MANAGEMENT

> *There is nothing either good or bad but thinking makes it so*
> William Shakespeare, *Hamlet*

FIVE STEPS TO EMOTIONAL INTELLIGENCE

STEP 2: EMOTION MANAGEMENT

Managing our emotions effectively involves controlling those unproductive behaviours that really don't get us anywhere. You might feel great at winning a shouting match with a difficult colleague or customer, but this is a short-term gain and transitory. You may have lost a potential major client and done nothing to build effective relationships. In addition, raising your adrenalin levels will do nothing for your longer-term health!

By understanding the link between your interpretation of an event and your responses to it, you can choose an alternative way to feel. This is a key EI capability. Using the feeling diary will help you to identify the interaction between your thoughts, feelings and actions.

FIVE STEPS TO EMOTIONAL INTELLIGENCE

STEP 2: EMOTION MANAGEMENT
THE DYNAMICS OF EMOTION

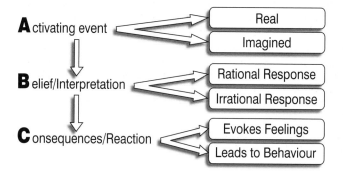

Activating event → Real / Imagined

Belief/Interpretation → Rational Response / Irrational Response

Consequences/Reaction → Evokes Feelings / Leads to Behaviour

THE FIVE STEPS TO EMOTIONAL INTELLIGENCE

STEP 2: EMOTION MANAGEMENT

As the Greek philosopher Epicletus said, *People are disturbed not only by things, but by the views they take of them*. What this means is that you can **choose** how you see a situation. For example, look at the picture on the next page: do you see an older lady or a young lady? Ask a colleague to look at the picture: do they see what you see?

Remember, our beliefs, values, drivers and the rules we live by create our map of reality. If we can begin to recognise the way in which we delete, distort and discount important information, and make decisions on the basis of little real evidence (simply our own perceptions) we can begin to see how much of our emotional life is influenced by our map of the world. Change the map and you change how you see, hear, feel and behave in the world.

You can change your interpretation of what you see and you can change your responses to it. No one can make us *feel* anything.

STEP 2: EMOTION MANAGEMENT

*Leeper's
ambiguous lady*

THE FIVE STEPS TO EMOTIONAL INTELLIGENCE

STEP 2: EMOTION MANAGEMENT
WORRY BUSTER TECHNIQUE

When you find yourself becoming anxious or angry, or become worried about undertaking some task (eg: a presentation) adopt the *worry buster* technique. Ask yourself the following questions:

- Where is the evidence for the way I am thinking?

- What is the logic in my interpretation?

- What do I have to lose if I do/say this?

- What do I have to gain if I do/say this?

- What would be the worst that could happen if I do/don't say or do this?

- What can I learn from saying/doing this?

THE FIVE STEPS TO EMOTIONAL INTELLIGENCE

STEP 2: EMOTION MANAGEMENT

APPLYING THE WORRY BUSTER TECHNIQUE

1. Specify the situation/problem or worry (in specific terms – only facts)
2. Ask yourself: *what is the worst that can happen?*
3. Ask yourself: *will it kill me?*
4. Write a statement resolving to accept the worst should it occur
5. Consider what specific steps you will take to begin immediately to improve upon the worst possible outcome

Learn to live with worries:
- Live one day at a time
- Get the facts
- Practise the worry buster technique
- Adopt the six-second rule

The six-second rule is so called because six seconds is the time it takes to capture the *flight* or *fight* response (ie: avoid the emotional hijacking). When someone has said or done something that triggers your hot button, take a deep breath and count six seconds before you respond. Just try it – what is the worst that can happen?

THE FIVE STEPS TO EMOTIONAL INTELLIGENCE

STEP 2: EMOTION MANAGEMENT
THE 5-STEP FREEZE-FRAME TECHNIQUE

Another method of exceptional emotion management is the 5-step freeze-frame technique:

1. Recognise stressful feelings and freeze-frame them. Take time out!

2. Make a concerted effort to shift your focus away from the racing mind or disturbing emotion(s).

3. Be calm and recall a positive, fun feeling that you have had and re-experience it.

4. Ask your heart, *What's a more effective response to this stressful situation?*

5. Listen and do what your heart says.

Source: Eq vs. IQ by Cynthia Kemper,
Communications World, 1999

THE FIVE STEPS TO EMOTIONAL INTELLIGENCE

STEP 3: SELF-MOTIVATION

THE FIVE STEPS TO EMOTIONAL INTELLIGENCE

STEP 3: SELF-MOTIVATION

Motivation comes from the Latin *to move*.
As human beings we are goal-oriented, and
being self-motivated means pursuing our goals
with commitment, passion, energy and persistence.

In order to achieve high levels of motivation,
overcome setbacks and perform at our best,
we need to be able to manage our own
internal states, harness our emotions and
channel them in a direction that enables
us to achieve our objectives.

YES
YES
I CAN
DO IT!

THE FIVE STEPS TO EMOTIONAL INTELLIGENCE

STEP 3: SELF-MOTIVATION

Being self-motivated calls for four essential actions. You can remember them by using the acronym **SAME**:

1. Adopt positive *Self-talk*
2. Build an effective support network (your '*A*' team*)
3. Visualise an inspirational *Mentor* (real or fictitious)
4. Create a conducive *Environment* (air, light, sound, visual images)

*Research shows that people with effective
'A' teams enjoy better psychological health and are
able to bounce back after setbacks.

THE FIVE STEPS TO EMOTIONAL INTELLIGENCE

STEP 3: SELF-MOTIVATION

ADOPT POSITIVE SELF-TALK

To develop an excellent inner-voice (positive self-talk) follow Janet's example:

Janet's goal is to feel better about herself, to increase her self-esteem. She, therefore, writes out the following:

I, Janet, am more and more pleasing to myself every day.
You, Janet, are more and more pleasing to yourself every day.
She, Janet, is more and more pleasing to herself every day.

I, Janet, am beginning to like myself as a woman.
You, Janet, are beginning to like yourself as a woman.
She, Janet, is beginning to like herself as a woman.

She writes out each affirmation three times, in the first, second and third persons. This is because our current views of ourselves are usually formed by a mixture of what we tell ourselves, what others tell us and what others say about us.

**Affirmations are always written in the positive sense, so there are no negatives –
not *I am not tense any more* but *I am relaxed*.**

THE FIVE STEPS TO EMOTIONAL INTELLIGENCE

STEP 3: SELF-MOTIVATION

 ADOPT POSITIVE SELF-TALK

Here are some suggested statements with which you can practise positive self-talk. Write in your own name and repeat the exercise in the second and third person.

I,	am beautiful and loveable
I,	am talented, intelligent and creative
I,	am growing cleverer every day
I,	have much to offer, and others recognise this
I,	am getting slimmer every day
I,	am getting on better with ... every day
I,	have a really beautiful nose
I,	have a lovely sense of humour that others appreciate very much
I,	am beginning to forgive ... for ...
I,	am getting over my disappointment at ...
I,	am working on that report so that it will be finished by ...
I,	am confident and can speak my mind clearly and confidently at meetings
I,	am becoming nicer every day
I,	am becoming happier every day

Alternatively you could read your affirmations into a tape and play it in your car, while in bed at night, or in the morning to wake you up – what a splendid way to start the day!

Source: adapted from *Managing Yourself*, Mike Pedler and Tom Boydell, 1999

STEP 3: SELF-MOTIVATION

 BUILD YOUR 'A' TEAM

To build an effective 'A' team, think about people who are in your current personal and organisational networks. Using the form below, write down the names of those colleagues, friends or associates who currently provide you with different kinds of support. If you have any gaps, you need to identify how these might be filled.

Types of support	At work	Away from work
Someone I can always rely on		
Someone I just enjoy chatting to		
Someone with whom I can discuss the exercises I am completing in this book		
Someone who makes me feel valued		
Someone who can give me honest feedback		
Someone who is always a valuable source of information		
Someone who will challenge me to sit up and take a good look at myself		
Someone I can depend on in a crisis		
Someone I feel close to		
Someone I can share bad news with		
Someone I can share good news and good feelings with		
Someone who introduces me to new ideas, new interests and new people		

THE FIVE STEPS TO EMOTIONAL INTELLIGENCE

STEP 3: SELF-MOTIVATION

VISUALISE AN INSPIRATIONAL MENTOR

Sports psychologists help successful athletes to use visualisation to enable them to create the right internal (mental) state in which to engage in their sport. Whether this is an image of winning a gold medal or breaking a *PB* (personal best) the aim is to achieve a state of *flow*. This is an internal state that energises and aligns emotions with the task in hand.

Two decades of research by the U.S. based psychologist Czikszentmihalyi show that activities that both challenge and permit us to draw on existing knowledge are most likely to send us into a state of *flow*. Daniel Goleman describes *flow* as the harnessing of our emotions to achieve superior performance and learning.

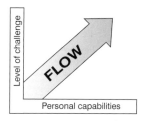

THE FIVE STEPS TO EMOTIONAL INTELLIGENCE

STEP 3: SELF-MOTIVATION

VISUALISE AN INSPIRATIONAL MENTOR

To visualise an inspirational figure (mentor):

1. Think of someone (either real or imaginary) whom you consider to be inspirational
    (eg: Martin Luther King, Mother Theresa, Capt. Scarlett).

2. Create an image of that person in your mind's eye at their most inspiring (eg: Martin
    Luther King's *I have a dream* speech).

3. Imagine they are on a TV screen, turn up the colour and sound so that you are able
    to experience the feelings that the scene evokes.

4. When the feelings are at their peak, introduce a key word, a touch or gesture that
    you can use as a trigger to conjure up the image and inspirational feelings
    associated with it.

5. Repeat a number of times to ensure that you are able to fire off this *anchor* when
    you need to be inspired.

6. Test out your visualisation and ask the following question: *If* (name of mentor)
    were here now, what would she/he/it say or do?

STEP 3: SELF-MOTIVATION

VISUALISE AN INSPIRATIONAL MENTOR

For some time we have been aware of the different functions of the left brain (logic, reason, maths, reading, language and analysis) and the right brain (recognition, rhythm, visual imagery, creativity, synthesis, dreams, symbols and emotions). Developing your emotional intelligence means accessing all of the psychic resources you have available.

Creative visualisation, using imagination, is a normal feature of the nervous system, which has largely been ignored for being labelled *unscientific*.

A central idea is that the brain when it creates an image (whether real or imaginary) gives rise to emotional states that will evoke behaviour. Changing the way you think will change the way you feel and, therefore, change the way you behave.

THE FIVE STEPS TO EMOTIONAL INTELLIGENCE

STEP 3: SELF-MOTIVATION

CREATE AN EI ENVIRONMENT

Think of a place where you were happiest. What did you see and hear? Was there plenty of light? Inspirational images? Identify what you need to have around you to make you feel motivated.

To create an environment that is conducive to developing high EI, make sure your environment meets the following criteria:

1. Healthy and helpful:
   - Is the air clean?
   - Can you hear helpful sounds?

2. Light:
   - Is it a motivator?

3. Contains motivators that you can surround yourself with, such as:
   - Pictures (Of your inspirational mentor, perhaps?)
   - People
   - Phrases

4. Organised:
   - Clear your desk, clear your mind

THE FIVE STEPS TO EMOTIONAL INTELLIGENCE

STEP 3: SELF-MOTIVATION

CREATE AN EI ENVIRONMENT

Research shows that music enhances performance. As the accelerated learning guru Dr Georgi Lazanov notes: *A well-executed concert can do about 60% of the presenting work in about 5% of the time.*

Students listening to Mozart for just 10 minutes prior to taking a SAT test raised their scores by an average 10-15 points!

Well-chosen music can lead to:
- Lower levels of stress
- Improvements in long-term memory and retention
- Higher levels of creativity
- Enhanced learning
- Desired emotional states (relaxed, energised, focused, cleansed, creative, uplifted)

For more information read *Tune Your Brain* by Elizabeth Miles, Berkeley Books, 1997

INTERPERSONAL INTELLIGENCE (STEPS 4 & 5)

This chapter continues with steps four and five on the pathway to EI. These final steps – *relationship management and emotion coaching* – are key to our interpersonal intelligence, the outer-intelligence we use to read, sense and understand, and manage our relationships with others.

THE FIVE STEPS TO EMOTIONAL INTELLIGENCE

STEP 4: RELATIONSHIP MANAGEMENT

> *The ways that people treat us are reflections of the ways we treat ourselves.*
> Linda Field, *The Self-Esteem Workbook*

STEP 4: RELATIONSHIP MANAGEMENT

My own research shows that relationships are vital for personal growth and development. Over the last decade of organisational restructuring, relationships between employer and employed have irrevocably changed.

Where once the *psychological contract* was based on such expectations as a job for life, this is now characterised by transactional relationships, which are transitory. Flatter organisational structures and the need to manage our own careers mean that developing an effective internal and external network of relationships is vital.

Relationship Management means being effective at managing relationships and building effective networks.

THE FIVE STEPS TO EMOTIONAL INTELLIGENCE

STEP 4: RELATIONSHIP MANAGEMENT

Defining a relationship: *The coming together of two or more people for their mutual benefit.*

Types of relationship:
- Personal partnerships
- Friendships
- Relationships with work colleagues

Reasons why we get together:
- Companionship
- Sense of belonging
- Establish a support system
- Build our identity
- Personal development
- Love
- Enhance a sense of common purpose
- Develop a sense of teamwork
- Produce a product or service

THE FIVE STEPS TO EMOTIONAL INTELLIGENCE

STEP 4: RELATIONSHIP MANAGEMENT

Reasons why relationships fail:

- Unrealistic expectations
- Lack of empathy
- Immaturity (low EI!)
- Dependency/co-dependency
- Inability to assert own needs
- Poor communication
- Ineffective strategies for conflict resolution
- Personality differences (different maps of the world)

57

THE FIVE STEPS TO EMOTIONAL INTELLIGENCE

STEP 4: RELATIONSHIP MANAGEMENT

What makes an effective relationship?

1. Reciprocity

This means meeting each other's needs: *You support – I support*. For example, if you repeatedly ask colleagues for help, advice or information, but do not find time to respond to their enquiries, eventually they will withhold their know-how and support. (Think how devastating this could be at an organisational level.) Often it is only in repeated interactions that we can begin to identify the real needs of an individual. Check out your perceptions (remember Leeper's Ambiguous Lady?).

2. Skills

- *Dynamic listening:* Actively listen by paying attention to both verbal and non-verbal cues to identify what is really being said/or not said.

- *Establish empathy:* Step into their shoes and tune into their language to access their map of reality.

- *Use questions:* Directly ask what an individual's needs are. Don't mind-read. Remember, to **ASSUME** is to make an **ASS** out of **U** and **ME**!

THE FIVE STEPS TO EMOTIONAL INTELLIGENCE

STEP 4: RELATIONSHIP MANAGEMENT

3. Relating over time

- *Continuity:* Build up a picture of the other person. See them in different situations and different contexts in order to gather clues about who the person is, their beliefs, values and hot buttons. This will help you to relate better.

- *Build trust:* Establishing rapport involves trust and comfort, both of which need to be nurtured. Learn from each interaction and use this new knowledge to ensure subsequent interactions are positive and productive.

4. Engage in exchange

To build an effective relationship, exchange factual information, thoughts, feelings and ideas. It is an interactive process: what you disclose has an impact on the other person, which affects how you respond. **Remember, the ways people treat us are reflections of the ways we treat ourselves. Relationships are not made outside, they are made inside.**

THE FIVE STEPS TO EMOTIONAL INTELLIGENCE

STEP 4: RELATIONSHIP MANAGEMENT

Tips for sharing thoughts, feelings and ideas:

- Be in a good frame of mind
- Tune into how the other person responds
- Set a positive tone to the discussion
- Check out any feelings of discomfort

Remember, when we communicate our emotions:

55% is non-verbal (through our body language)
38% is the tone of voice
7% is dependent on the content (the actual words we use)

> ***It ain't what you say, it's the way that you say it!***
> 1980s pop band Fun Boy Three

THE FIVE STEPS TO EMOTIONAL INTELLIGENCE

STEP 4: RELATIONSHIP MANAGEMENT

Six steps to building effective relationships:

1. Know the boundaries of the relationships (what can and can't be said or done; behaviours that are acceptable outside of work may be inappropriate within the workplace)
2. Check out expectations (respective needs and wants)
3. Review your perceptions (avoid making assumptions on basis of little evidence)
4. Review the other person's perceptions of you (take a risk, ask yourself what is the worst that can happen – use the *worry buster* to help)
5. Examine interactions (consider what worked well or not so well, and why this might be the case)
6. Determine the desired outcomes (set exceptional goals that have **power**)

THE FIVE STEPS TO EMOTIONAL INTELLIGENCE

STEP 4: RELATIONSHIP MANAGEMENT

Top ten tips for building exceptional relationships with colleagues at work:

1. Appreciate their individual skills, knowledge and capabilities
2. Make time to get to know them and actively listen to what they have to say
3. Remember, you can have a good relationship without having to be their bosom pals
4. If you have a disagreement with someone, look for an early solution
5. Spend some social time as well as work time with them
6. Give positive feedback for a job well done (as Manuel London of AT&T once said, *without feedback there is no learning*)
7. Seek their advice and opinions whenever you can
8. Support them through the tough times
9. Recognise individual uniqueness, be flexible in your style and approach, understand their *map of reality*
10. Use common courtesies and friendly greetings (research shows that leaders have a powerful impact on the emotional climate within a workgroup; being miserable can be contagious!)

THE FIVE STEPS TO EMOTIONAL INTELLIGENCE

STEP 4: RELATIONSHIP MANAGEMENT

FINAL THOUGHT

Most people who work have to work with other people. No matter how enjoyable a job is, it can become stressful and unfulfilling or downright miserable if human relationships break down. The first thing to realise and accept is that you cannot change other people. All you can do is to change yourself.

When someone says or does something to annoy you, *the annoyance is not in the thing being done, but in your response to the thing that is being done.* Things and actions are not in themselves annoying: the annoyance lies within ourselves, in the response.

> *If you keep on doing what you have always done, you will keep on getting what you have always got!*

STEP 5: EMOTION COACHING

> *Managers need to change their whole approach to managing and instead of relying on systems and control procedures, need to get to know and trust their people as individuals ... Direct personal contact and coaching keeps managers appraised of real business challenges and provides an opportunity to shape responses through a shared understanding. The new corporation is the individualised corporation.*

S. Goshal & C. Bartlett, *Harvard Business Review*, May-June 1995

THE FIVE STEPS TO EMOTIONAL INTELLIGENCE

STEP 5: EMOTION COACHING

The fifth and final step: learning to become an emotion coach (E-coach), an important EI capability.

The changing shape of organisations means that we need new types of leaders. As Pat Fritts observes, *Organisations need emotionally intelligent managers, who will help to develop the competencies and commitment to work together in the new knowledge economy.*

In terms of EI, being an E-coach means helping others to:
- Develop their emotional capabilities
- Resolve differences
- Solve problems
- Communicate effectively
- Become motivated

My own research shows the importance of 1:1 support in developing both individual and team EI capabilities. The growth in the popularity of coaching means that this 5th and final step is a crucial capability and a measure of an effective coach.

THE FIVE STEPS TO EMOTIONAL INTELLIGENCE

STEP 5: EMOTION COACHING
E-COACH CAPABILITIES

To become an exceptionally EI coach you need to *know:*

- What coaching means (as distinct from other learning roles)
- What the coaching process entails and what relevant models to use
- How to manage the relationship and agree the boundaries
- Where coaching fits within the overall scheme of things (if part of an organisational programme)
- How people respond to change and how to overcome resistance to change
- How people learn and how to assess differences in learning styles
- How to apply different psychological models and ways of assessing values, beliefs, motivation, personality (and emotional intelligence)
- What competencies need to be developed, either personally or for a specific job role

THE FIVE STEPS TO EMOTIONAL INTELLIGENCE

STEP 5: EMOTION COACHING

E-COACH CAPABILITIES

What *skills* do you need to become an exceptionally EI coach? You need to:

- Actively listen (to what is being said and not said – use your intuition)
- Use different questioning techniques to get beneath the surface and challenge the underlying problem, not the surface issue
- Influence, persuade and challenge (knowing when to adopt different styles)
- Engage in problem-solving and use creativity techniques to help the learner *think outside of the box*
- Have good time/personal management skills
- Help the learner to set goals and identify possible strategies
- Network and access resources that will help the learner
- Help the learner to put together an Action Plan, to identify enablers and disablers towards achieving their goals

THE FIVE STEPS TO EMOTIONAL INTELLIGENCE

STEP 5: EMOTION COACHING
E-COACH CAPABILITIES

What *behaviours* do you need to demonstrate? You need to:

- Demonstrate empathy and capacity to build rapport
- Act as an EI role model
- Be non-judgemental
- Maintain confidentiality
- Signpost learner to other sources of support (recognising your own limitations and gaps in learning)
- Continually engage in a critical evaluation of your own performance and take action
- Be committed to your own personal and on-going development
- Continually seek to build learner's confidence and self-esteem, to open their horizons

THE FIVE STEPS TO EMOTIONAL INTELLIGENCE

STEP 5: EMOTION COACHING

E-COACH CAPABILITIES

What *qualities* and *experiences* should you possess? You should have:

- Experience of supporting learners
- Experience of being coached or mentored
- A sense of humour
- Tact and diplomacy
- Ability to demonstrate integrity
- Capacity to show evidence of persistence and resilience
- A willingness to share own learning experiences (successes and failures)
- Confidence in your own abilities
- Passion when embracing your role as E-coach
- Capability to be congruent, journeying along your *path with a heart*
- Emotional intelligence!

THE FIVE STEPS TO EMOTIONAL INTELLIGENCE

STEP 5: EMOTION COACHING
ROLE OF THE E-COACH

There has been an explosion in approaches to coaching, with everyone claiming to offer the ideal model to help people achieve their personal, professional and life goals. (You may find *The Coaching and Buying Coaching Services* report on www.cipd.co.uk a useful resource).

In practical terms you need to use a model or framework that addresses four key elements:

1. An assessment of where the learner is now
2. Identification of where the learner wants to get to
3. Planning how to get there
4. Feedback on results

Whenever I work with individuals I use an 8-step model that can be remembered by using the following phrase: ***D**on't **A**gree **A**nything **A**t **A**nytime **A**ccept **A**ll **R**ewards*. An explanation of the eight steps follows.

THE FIVE STEPS TO EMOTIONAL INTELLIGENCE

STEP 5: EMOTION COACHING

ROLE OF THE E-COACH

1. Diagnosis

Here I meet with the learner and their sponsor to:

- Establish benchmarks and objectives for the programme. Typically, assignments include: coaching for skills and performance; coaching for career development and personal growth; coaching for life/work balance

- Give the individual a questionnaire to complete. The person is asked to rate themselves as to where they are now along a set of personal, professional and emotional competencies and where they need to be.

- Agree a *coaching contract* between the learner and organisational sponsor. This specifies the outcomes of the programme and what support will be provided (by the coach, the individual and the organisation) and the confidentiality aspect.

It is also important at this stage to gauge whether there is the right *chemistry* between us. Without it I know the process just won't work! Also, it is important to agree what and how much information is to be given to the sponsor. The line I usually take (and to which organisations agree) is as follows: *I will get the client to London, but the route we take is between me and the learner!*

THE FIVE STEPS TO EMOTIONAL INTELLIGENCE

STEP 5: EMOTION COACHING

ROLE OF THE E-COACH

2. Alliance
This is the first meeting during which:
- The purpose of the coaching is outlined
- A clear set of objectives is agreed (using **POSIE**)
- Specific assessment tools are identified

3. Assessment
Here an audit is undertaken of existing and desired competencies, strengths and weaknesses. As the E-coach, I:
- Use plenty of open questions
- Reflect and summarise to help the learner explore themselves and begin to develop their self-awareness
- Use particular psychometric tools and other exercises which might include: career and interest inventories; personal and working styles; personality questionnaires; and, if the assignment is specifically designed to develop EI capabilities, specific EQ measures such as the Boston EIQ (version 2) both self-report and 360-degree feedback

The key is to use tools that are appropriate for the task. It is like selecting the right drill bit for the size of hole you wish to create!

THE FIVE STEPS TO EMOTIONAL INTELLIGENCE

STEP 5: EMOTION COACHING
ROLE OF THE E-COACH

4. Analysis
During this session the learner and I:
- Use assessment information to identify existing capabilities and prioritise development areas, using such frameworks as SWOT (Strengths/Weaknesses/Opportunities/Threats)
- Discuss appropriate models or competency frameworks (eg: *5-steps to EI*)
- Prioritise development actions

5. Alternatives
Here we:
- Consider alternative ways in which to work on development areas
- Use problem-solving strategies to explore options and possibilities (enablers and disablers)
- Use a structured process for decision-making – checking out what is realistic and practical

THE FIVE STEPS TO EMOTIONAL INTELLIGENCE

STEP 5: EMOTION COACHING
ROLE OF THE E-COACH

6. Action Planning
Here we:
- Devise a detailed plan
- Identify sources of support/hindrance
- Agree timescales

It is important as the E-coach to use a mix of confrontation and support, to help the individual take the necessary actions and avoid procrastination.

7. Application
Here the learner undertakes the actions agreed, which may include:
- Behavioural exercises (doing something different, like communicating with a colleague in a different way, chairing a meeting, physically walking-the-job)
- Reading articles/books on issues that are relevant to the development plan
- Exercises such as life/career essay; personal and career evaluations
- Relaxation techniques
- Keeping a feeling diary

THE FIVE STEPS TO EMOTIONAL INTELLIGENCE

STEP 5: EMOTION COACHING

ROLE OF THE E-COACH

8. Review, Feedback and Evaluation

Here the learner:

- Discusses thoughts, feelings and outcomes of actions undertaken
- Identifies what worked well and not so well
- Explores key learning points
- Agrees further development actions with the coach

At the end of the programme, evaluation of outcomes is carried out between coach and learner, coach and sponsor, and learner and sponsor.

THE FIVE STEPS TO EMOTIONAL INTELLIGENCE

STEP 5: EMOTION COACHING
ROLE OF THE E-COACH

You can use this 8-step framework for the coaching programme and for individual sessions, thus meeting essential key elements of:

1.   An assessment of where the learner is now
2.   Identification of where the learner wants to get to
3.   Planning how to get there
4.   Feedback on results

Remember:
IQ + E-coaching = Competencies + EI = Performance, Productivity and Prosperity

ASSESSING & DEVELOPING
YOUR EMOTIONAL
<u>INTELLIGENCE</u>

ASSESSING YOUR EMOTIONAL INTELLIGENCE

Having introduced the 5-step model for developing EI, now is a useful point at which to establish just where you are on an EI scale. Complete the Boston EIQ (short version) to assess your current level of EI and identify those capabilities that you need to work on. Use the EI development plan (on page 85) to help you focus your energies. Find a coach; take action; use the exercises in this book and then afterwards re-assess your EI.

My own research and work developing EI with individuals and teams shows that enhancing EI capabilities is dependent upon a coach – just take a look at what the England football and rugby teams have achieved through having their own *emotionally intelligent* coaches!

Enjoy the journey!

ASSESSING & DEVELOPING YOUR EMOTIONAL INTELLIGENCE

THE BOSTON EI QUESTIONNAIRE

The following questions are designed to help you establish just how aware you are of your emotional responses and how well you use your emotional intelligence.

The questionnaire follows the 5-step model of EI. For each question tick the box that comes closest to how you feel about the answer.

	A	B	C	D
1. Can you tell when your mood is changing?	Always	Sometimes	Rarely	Never
2. Do you know when you are becoming defensive?	Always	Sometimes	Rarely	Never
3. Can you tell when your emotions are affecting your performance?	Always	Sometimes	Rarely	Never
4. How quickly do you realise you are starting to lose your temper?	Very quickly	Not very quickly	Slowly	Very slowly
5. How soon do you realise that your thoughts are turning negative?	Straightaway	Quite soon	After a while	Usually too late

THE BOSTON EI QUESTIONNAIRE

	A	B	C	D
6. Can you relax when you are under pressure?	Very easily	Quite easily	Hardly ever	Not at all
7. Do you *just get on with things* when you are angry?	Usually	Sometimes	Not usually	Never
8. Do you engage in *self-talk* to vent feelings of anger or anxiety?	Often	Sometimes	Rarely	Never
9. Do you remain cool in the face of others' anger or aggression?	Always	Usually	Occasionally	Never
10. How well can you concentrate when you are feeling anxious?	Very well	Quite well	Just about	Not at all

ASSESSING & DEVELOPING YOUR EMOTIONAL INTELLIGENCE

THE BOSTON EI QUESTIONNAIRE

	A	B	C	D
11. Do you *bounce back* quickly after a setback?	Always	Sometimes	Occasionally	Never
12. Do you deliver on your promises?	Without fail	Quite often	Rarely	Never
13. Can you *kick start* yourself into action when appropriate?	Yes, always	Yes, sometimes	Not often	No, never
14. How willingly do you change the way you do things when current methods are not working?	Very willingly	Quite willingly	Quite reluctantly	Very reluctantly
15. Are you able to lift your energy level to tackle and complete *boring tasks*?	Always	Usually	Rarely	Never

81

THE BOSTON EI QUESTIONNAIRE

	A	B	C	D
16. Do you actively seek ways of resolving conflict?	Yes, often	Yes, sometimes	Not often	Never
17. To what extent do you influence others about the way things are done?	A great extent	To some extent	Very little	None
18. How willing are you to act as a spokesperson for others?	Very willing	Can be persuaded	Quite reluctantly	Not at all willing
19. Are you able to demonstrate empathy with others' feelings?	Always	Sometimes	Rarely	Never
20. To what extent do you find that others trust and confide in you?	Frequently	Occasionally	Hardly ever	Never

THE BOSTON EI QUESTIONNAIRE

	A	B	C	D
21. Do you find yourself able to raise morale and make others feel good?	Yes, often	Yes, sometimes	Rarely	Never
22. How freely do you offer help and assistance to others?	Very freely	Quite freely	Reluctantly	Not freely at all
23. Can you sense when others are feeling angry or anxious and respond appropriately?	Yes, always	Yes, often	Hardly ever	Never
24. How effective are you at communicating your feelings to others?	Very	Quite	Not very	Not at all
25. Do you contribute to the management of conflict and emotion within your work group or family?	Yes, often	Yes, sometimes	Rarely	Never

ASSESSING & DEVELOPING YOUR EMOTIONAL INTELLIGENCE

THE BOSTON EI QUESTIONNAIRE

MARKING YOUR ANSWERS

Give yourself 4 points for each box ticked in column A, 3 points for each box ticked in column B, 2 for C and 1 for D. Enter the scores in the boxes below and fill in the totals.

Question					
1	2	3	4	5	**Total** (Questions 1-5)
☐	☐	☐	☐	☐	☐ Your score for **Self-awareness**
6	7	8	9	10	**Total** (Questions 6-10)
☐	☐	☐	☐	☐	☐ Your score for **Emotion management**
11	12	13	14	15	**Total** (Questions 11-15)
☐	☐	☐	☐	☐	☐ Your score for **Self-motivation**
16	17	18	19	20	**Total** (Questions 16-20)
☐	☐	☐	☐	☐	☐ Your score for **Relationship management**
21	22	23	24	25	**Total** (Questions 21-25)
☐	☐	☐	☐	☐	☐ Your score for **Emotion coaching**

If you scored 17 or more on any dimension you seem to shape up pretty well. A score of 13 to 16 indicates some remedial work is necessary. 12 to 9 *roll up your sleeves*. 8 or less means *oh dear*! But do not despair whatever your score. Now that you understand emotional intelligence you will be able to develop your own EI.

EI DEVELOPMENT PLAN

5 steps to emotional intelligence	My EI development goal(s) are (using POSIE)	How am I going to achieve my goal(s)? Development actions	What do I need to help me? Support/ resources	When am I going to achieve my goal(s) Time-scales
1. Self-awareness				
2. Emotion management				
3. Self-motivation				
4. Relationship management				
5. Emotion coaching				

WHAT CAN I DO TO RAISE MY EI?

- The first step is to identify your own emotions. (Use the feeling word list opposite to help you.)

- Take responsibility for them. (This is much harder.)

- Learn what compassion and empathy are. (This is much easier if you have taken the first two steps; impossible if you haven't!)

- Read books on emotions. (Consult the *mind, body & soul* section of any good book shop.)

- Get involved with learning, Continuous Professional Development or other networks.

- Find a quiet place/time to express your feelings. Keep a feeling journal.

- Read emotional literature, watch emotional movies, label the feelings being acted out. (Soaps are a good source for the full continuum of human emotions!)

- Avoid people who invalidate you.

SOME *FEELING WORDS*

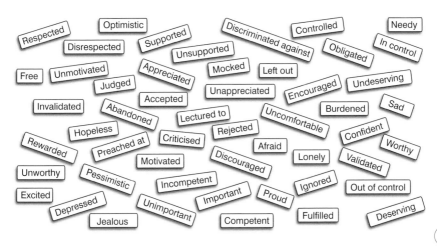

ASSESSING & DEVELOPING YOUR EMOTIONAL INTELLIGENCE

TEN HABITS OF EMOTIONALLY INTELLIGENT PEOPLE

People with high EI:

1. Label their feelings, rather than labelling people or situations
2. Distinguish between thoughts and feelings
3. Take responsibility for their feelings
4. Use their emotions to help make decisions
5. Show respect for others' feelings
6. Feel energised, not angry
7. Validate others' feelings
8. Practise getting a positive value from their negative emotions
9. Don't advise, command, control, criticise, blame or judge others
10. Avoid people who invalidate them or don't respect their feelings

DEVELOPING AN EMOTIONALLY INTELLIGENT ORGANISATION

DEVELOPING AN EMOTIONALLY INTELLIGENT ORGANISATION

> *Top down, corporate-wide organisation development is becoming less consistent with contemporary organisational forms. The requirement on managers to deal effectively with more complex organisations places a greater premium on individual contribution, which in turn relies on meta-abilities...individual development is the starting point for organisation development.*
>
> Cranfield University, 1997

> *Leadership is about emotion.*
>
> Hooper & Potter, The Business of Leadership, 1997

EI AS A CHANGE MANAGEMENT STRATEGY

So far in this book I have looked at ways in which you can develop your own EI. This is the fundamental starting point for developing an EI organisation. This is leadership development from the inside-out, not outside-in like much training that managers participate in!

I have offered evidence to justify the hard case for soft skills. In this final section of the book I am going to help those of you who want to use EI as a change management strategy.

I shall be drawing on the experience of what two U.S. writers, Cary Cherniss and Mitchel Adler, have identified as what works best. This is based on a 4-step model that you can remember through the phrase: *Some People Take the Micky*

1. **S**ecure commitment
2. **P**repare for change
3. **T**rain & develop
4. **M**aintain & evaluate

This is illustrated in the diagram on page 92, which I will now take you through.

EI AS A CHANGE MANAGEMENT STRATEGY

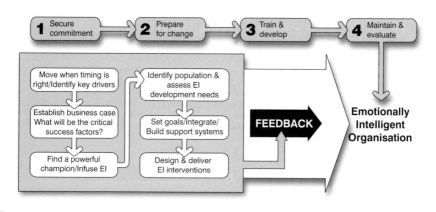

1 Secure commitment → 2 Prepare for change → 3 Train & develop → 4 Maintain & evaluate

Move when timing is right/Identify key drivers

Establish business case What will be the critical success factors?

Find a powerful champion/Infuse EI

Identify population & assess EI development needs

Set goals/Integrate/ Build support systems

Design & deliver EI interventions

FEEDBACK

Emotionally Intelligent Organisation

DEVELOPING AN EMOTIONALLY INTELLIGENT ORGANISATION

STEP 1: SECURE COMMITMENT

Get *buy-in* by answering the following questions:
- What are the key drivers or triggers for change, what *pain* exists within the business?
- How can EI help?
- What are the hot buttons for top management?
- Who are the key stakeholders and what's in it for them (WIFT)?
- What are the added value or bottom-line benefits for developing EI capabilities?
- How will you establish the critical success factors?
- Who has high EI and can champion the programme?
- Who is going to design the programme?
- How will EI be communicated or infused within the organisation?

Possible reasons for developing EI include:
- Lost productivity through low morale
- High turnover of staff
- Need to attract and retain talent
- Enable employees to achieve work/life balance
- Reduce organisational stress
- Improve client relationships
- Enhance leadership capability and potential
- Address outcomes from organisational DNA (Development Needs Assessment)

STEP 2: PREPARE FOR CHANGE

Having established the business case you now need to:
- Identify what EI capabilities need to be developed and are critical for successful performance
- Conduct a gap analysis between any existing competency frameworks and EI capabilities
- Assess EI development needs
- Identify possible participants
- Gauge readiness of the learners

Remember: EI is *inside-out* development and needs personal commitment. As the popular saying goes, *How many psychologists does it take to change a light bulb? Well, it doesn't matter how many, but the light bulb has got to really, really, really want to change!*

You also need to establish:
- How the facilitators will convince learners that EI capabilities can be developed
- How the facilitators will demonstrate the WIFM factor to get individual buy-in
- The nature of and commitment to on-going support

DEVELOPING AN EMOTIONALLY INTELLIGENT ORGANISATION

STEP 2: PREPARE FOR CHANGE
CONDUCTING A COMPETENCY GAP ANALYSIS (CGA)

1. Do your homework, read around EI and understand what emotional capabilities mean and how they can make a difference (see *further reading* at end of book)
2. Review your existing competency frameworks and examine how EI capabilities *map* onto your existing models; you may like to use the following:

Our Competency	Self-awareness (knowing one's own internal states, preferences, resources & intuitions)	Our Competency	Self-management (managing one's own internal states, impulses & resources)
	Emotional awareness: recognising one's emotions & their effects		Self-control: keeping disruptive emotions & impulses in check
	Accurate self-assessment: knowing your strengths/limitations		Achievement drive: striving to improve or meet a standard of excellence; persistence in pursuing goals despite obstacles
	Self-confidence: a strong sense of self-worth		Conscientiousness & reliability: taking responsibility for personal performance; maintaining standards of honesty & integrity
			Adaptability: flexibility in handling change initiative & innovation
			Readiness to act on opportunities; being comfortable with novel ideas, approaches & information

Mapping existing competencies against EI dimensions

3. Identify those meta-EI capabilities that will differentiate star performers
4. Gain commitment and *buy-in* from all stakeholders
5. Communicate   6. Develop   7. Evaluate

DEVELOPING AN EMOTIONALLY INTELLIGENT ORGANISATION

STEP 3: TRAIN & DEVELOP

In designing and delivering the EI intervention you need to ask yourself:

- Who is best placed to facilitate?

- What resources are available?

- Do the facilitators display the necessary emotional competencies?

- How will I ensure that they do?

- What will be included in the design and how much time will be spent on cognitive vs experiential activities?

- How will real-time feedback be incorporated and handled?

- How will EI capabilities be practised back *on the job*?

As I noted earlier, *Without feedback there is no learning*. So, who is going to provide the support, what form of support will this be and how will you ensure this will happen?

DEVELOPING AN EMOTIONALLY INTELLIGENT ORGANISATION

STEP 3: TRAIN & DEVELOP
ELEMENTS OF AN EFFECTIVE EI DEVELOPMENT PROGRAMME

Developing emotional capabilities means unlearning old habits of thought, feeling and action. It also involves commitment, motivation, sustained effort and practice. Kate Cannon, designer of American Express's EI programme, advocates three simple principles:

1. **Theory**
   Background to EI and why it is important to develop it within the organisation

2. **Practice**
   Introduce core EI skills and allow learners to practise, practise, practise

3. **Application**
   Support for learners to apply the tools back on-the-job

DEVELOPING AN EMOTIONALLY INTELLIGENT ORGANISATION

STEP 3: TRAIN & DEVELOP
ELEMENTS OF AN EFFECTIVE EI DEVELOPMENT PROGRAMME

Tips for design:

- Use multi-sensory methods and media (music, pictures, stories, poetry) that tap into multiple intelligences

- Appeal to different learning styles and preferences

- Stage the training over a number of weeks

- Use small groups (established teams work best)

- Ensure learners practise during and between sessions and after formal training is complete

- Incorporate *real-time* and on-going feedback

- Allow for some *down-time* for learners to reflect on their own responses and those of others

- Incorporate assignments that can be integrated back on-the-job

- Use tips and techniques suggested in this book!

DEVELOPING AN EMOTIONALLY INTELLIGENT ORGANISATION

STEP 4: MAINTAIN & EVALUATE

Following the intervention, you need to make sure that:

1. There is on-going coaching and support
2. Coaches are trained
3. Other people management and development strategies encourage the improvement of EI capabilities
4. Line managers are involved and *buy-in* to the process is gained
5. EI capabilities are not just an add-on but are regarded as the core capabilities for successful performance
6. EI intervention is evaluated against established benchmarks (the critical success factors)

DEVELOPING AN EMOTIONALLY INTELLIGENT ORGANISATION

STEP 4: MAINTAIN & EVALUATE

EVALUATING EI DEVELOPMENT

Kirkpatrick's (1967) model for training evaluation is useful here:

1. **Immediate reaction:** post-training feedback sheets (happy sheets) to gauge learner's satisfaction with programme
2. **Learning:** pre- and post-development assessments (ideally 360° EI feedback)
3. **Behaviour:** manager appraisals of individual performance
4. **Business performance:** assessment against original critical success factors/benchmarks for EI

For wider programme evaluation:

- Establish *control* group (to compare performance of participants who have been through the programme, with that of similar group who haven't)
- Undertake validation study of EI competencies
- Carry out qualitative evaluation (often referred to as *illuminative evaluation*) to identify individual and organisational benefits from EI intervention
- Review outcomes and re-design

DEVELOPING AN EMOTIONALLY INTELLIGENT ORGANISATION

EXAMPLE EI DEVELOPMENT PROGRAMME

Group size	16
Group characteristics	Established team
Structure	1 day a month for 5 months
Topics	• EI, what is it? • EI capabilities in relation to existing management competencies • Building a vision, eliciting values and setting powerful goals • Building effective relationships • Correcting faulty thinking (reframing using ABC) • Monitoring self in action • Identifying past patterns (negative self-talk & outdated tapes)

Media & methods	• Cognitive & experiential learning • Role plays, feedback • Peer E-coaching • Action learning • Music • Metaphors • ABC/Freeze-frame • Pairs/Self-disclosure • Personal action planning • Behavioural assignments
Support	• Managers trained as E-coaches
Evaluation	• Happy sheets • Pre- and post- 360° EI questionnaires (Boston EIQ) • Performance appraisals • Illuminative evaluation 1 year after initial programme

FINAL THOUGHTS & REFLECTIONS

There are links between the internal life of emotions and political and social issues which, if explored, would contribute to the transformation of society for which so many yearn. Emotional literacy generates a sense of meaning, not only in private but also in public life.
Andrew Samuels, Co-Founder of Antidote:
Campaign for an Emotionally Literate Society, 2000

In the 1980s there was a culture of me, me, me and greed is good … this no longer holds true … everything is changing and I think corporations are recognising that. What we are now recognising is that, to be successful (and profitable) we need to get back in touch with what matters to individuals, how individuals react, talk and walk with each other … and to harness the feelgood factor to persuade people to do business with us.

EI … is an evolutionary path towards getting a blend between individuals acting and executing tasks in a particular way, with a spirit that pervades everything that the organisation does … it is about getting people in the organisation to deliver the corporate values, to feel good about themselves, about each other and more importantly, to project that passion to sell products in a sincere way.
Senior executive, global financial services organisation, 2001

FURTHER READING

On Emotional Intelligence

David Caruso & Peter Salovey,
The Emotionally Intelligent Manager,
Jossey-Bass (2004)

Professional Journals:
*Competency & Emotional Intelligence Quarterly:
The Journal of Performance Through People*
(www.irseclipse.co.uk)

Cary Cherniss & Mitchel Adler,
Promoting Emotional Intelligence in Organizations,
American Society of Training & Development (2000)
(access via amazon.com).

Dr Malcolm Higgs & Prof. V. Dulewicz,
Making Sense of Emotional Intelligence,
NFER-NELSON (1999)

Daniel Goleman,
Working with Emotional Intelligence,
Bloomsbury (1998).

Daniel Goleman, Richard Boyatzis
& Annie McKee,
The New Leaders, Little, Brown (2002).

Dr. Hendrie Weisinger,
Emotional Intelligence at Work,
Jossey-Bass (1998).

Doc Childre & Howard Martin,
*The Heartmath Solution: Proven techniques
for Developing Emotional Intelligence*,
Piatkus, 1999.

Patricia McBride & Susan Maitland,
*The EI Advantage: Putting Emotional
Intelligence into Practice*,
McGraw Hill, 2002.

FURTHER READING

Coaching, Coaching Psychology & Mentoring

Ian McDermott & Wendy Jargo,
The NLP Coach, Piatkus (2001).

Patrick E. Merlevede & Denis Bridoux,
*Mastering Mentoring and Coaching with
Emotional Intelligence: Increase Your Job EQ*,
Anglo-American Books (2004).

Gillian Burn,
The NLP Pocketbook,
Management Pocketbooks (2005).

Ian Fleming & Allan J.D. Taylor,
The Coaching Pocketbook,
Management Pocketbooks (2003).

Suzanne Skiffington & Perry Zeus,
Behavioral Coaching,
McGraw-Hill (2003).

David Megginson & David Clutterbuck,
Techniques for coaching and mentoring,
Elsevier, Butterworth/Heinemann (2005).

John Whitmore,
Coaching for Performance,
Nicholas Brealey (2002).

Anthony M. Grant & Jane Greene,
Coach Yourself: make real change in your life,
Pearson Education Ltd, 2001.

Joseph O'Connor & John Seymour,
Introducing Neuro-Linguistic Progamming (NLP),
Thorsons Audio.

Joseph O'Connor,
NLP Workbook,
Thorsons, 2001.

Useful Websites

www.antidote.org.uk
www.associationforcoaching.com
www.eiconsortium.org

EI RESOURCES

EQ ASSESSMENT TOOLS

Since this book appeared in 2001, writing in 2006 I can report that there has been an explosion in the number of practitioners offering EI interventions, often based around a single model of EQ. What this means in practice is that you really need to look at what is on offer. In studying this field for a decade, what I have learnt is that measures are based on the differing ways in which psychologists define EI. So ask yourself what is a particular tool measuring and what are you going to use the data for? Is it personal development? As a basis for raising leadership performance? Or, as part of a coaching intervention? Make sure that whatever your choice, it is 'fit for a purpose'. Ones that have been founded on sound research include:

- Bar-On Emotional Quotient Inventory (www.mhs.com)
- Emotional Competence Inventory (ei.haygroup.com)
- Boston EI-Q (www.eicoaching.co.uk)
- Individual and Team Effectiveness Questionnaires (www.jca.biz)

EI RESOURCES

EQ DEVELOPMENT

Over the last five years I have been pleased at the number of people who have used this book across the world, as a basis for EQ development. There are plenty of events ranging from half-day to in-depth programmes to develop professionals' capacity to operate as EI practitioners. In addition, most leadership competency frameworks now incorporate EI and use coaching to underpin behavioural change.

What I want to do here is to signpost you to some useful resources and organisations to help you to develop further your own EQ and that of others:

- The Centre for Applied Emotional Intelligence (www.emotionalintelligence.co.uk)
- Chartered Institute of Personnel & Development (www.cipd.co.uk)
- Division of Occupational Psychology, BPS (www.bps.org.uk)

To help design your own programmes:
- *Using Emotional Intelligence at Work and Developing An Emotionally Intelligent Team* (www.fenman.co.uk)
- *Emotional Intelligence in Action:* Training and Coaching Activities for leaders and managers (Hughes, Patterson & Terrell 2005) based on Bar-On model (www.pfeiffer.com)
- The Training Shop (www.thetrainingshop.co.uk)
- Management Learning Resources (www.mlr.co.uk)

About the Author

Margaret Chapman, C.Psychol, AFBPsS, Chartered FCIPD, FMAC Accredited Mediator, Master Practitioner NLP

Margaret has been working in the field of EI for nearly a decade. She has published and presented her work nationally and internationally and is regularly consulted by organisations to help them to design and evaluate EI interventions.

As an EI practitioner and behavioural coach Margaret draws on a wide range of approaches that have a sound psychological basis as to what works. These include NLP, cognitive-behavioural, solution-focused and existential. Her work in EI also involves working as a mediator to help address relationship and change management issues. Margaret co-designed the Boston EI-Q and is also an accredited user and trainer of the Bar-On EQ-I along with a number of other psychometric tools.

Contact
For more information about her work Margaret can be contacted at mc@eicoaching.co.uk

ORDER FORM

Your details

Name _____

Position _____

Company _____

Address _____

_____

_____

Telephone _____

Fax _____

E-mail _____

VAT No. (EC companies) _____

Your Order Ref _____

Please send me:

		No. copies
The Emotional Intelligence Pocketbook		
The _____ Pocketbook		
The _____ Pocketbook		
The _____ Pocketbook		
The _____ Pocketbook		

Order by Post
MANAGEMENT POCKETBOOKS LTD
LAUREL HOUSE, STATION APPROACH,
ALRESFORD, HAMPSHIRE SO24 9JH UK

Order by Phone, Fax or Internet
Telephone: +44 (0)1962 735573
Facsimile: +44 (0)1962 733637
E-mail: sales@pocketbook.co.uk
Web: www.pocketbook.co.uk

MANAGEMENT POCKETBOOKS